DIARY OF A GOD-MAN
CHILDREN'S LITURGY

created by kids for kids

YEAR C

PREACHED PRESS

PUBLISHER'S NOTE

Diary of a God-Man, all versions, is a work of personal inspiration, providing text and illustrations for children in a series covering the liturgical year.

Link to website and other info:
www.diaryofagodman.com
godman82020@gmail.com
@diary_of_a_godman -
Instagram @DiaryofaGodMan -
Facebook

Published and printed in the United States of America

PREACHED PRESS

Available in print and digital from Amazon

Fall Ordinary Time Year C

Dedication

We dedicate this book to God, our Father who is one with Jesus the God-Man and the Holy Spirit. It is wonderful to know we are created and loved by our Father who art in Heaven!

"Every good endowment and every perfect gift is from above,
coming down from the Father of lights
with whom there is no variation or shadow due to change.
Of his own will he brought us forth by the word of truth
that we should be a kind of first fruits of his creatures."
James 1:17-18

"God loves us more than a father, mother, friend, or any else could love,
and even more than we are able to love ourselves"
St. John Chrysostom

"In that same hour Jesus rejoiced int the Holy Spirit and said,
"I thank you, Father, Lord of heaven and earth,
that you have hidden these things from the wise and understanding
and revealed them to infants;
yes, Father for such was your gracious will."
Luke 10:21

CAN YOU FIND THESE GENEROUS SUPPORTERS IN THE BOOK?

DIARY OF A GOD-MAN CHARACTERS

Isaac

Jacob

Joshua

Lazarus

Michael

Moses

Naaman

Onesimus

Paul

Philemon

Raphael

Timothy

Zacchaeus

TABLE OF CONTENTS

ORDINARY TIME

ORDINARY TIME

WIS 9:13-18B

1ST READING

TWENTY-THIRD SUNDAY OF ORDINARY TIME

Who can know God's counsel,
or who can conceive what the LORD intends?
For the deliberations of mortals are timid,
and unsure are our plans.
For the corruptible body burdens the soul
and the earthen shelter weighs down the mind that has many concerns.
And scarce do we guess the things on earth,
and what is within our grasp we find with difficulty;
but when things are in heaven, who can search them out?
Or who ever knew your counsel, except you had given wisdom
and sent your holy spirit from on high?
And thus were the paths of those on earth made straight.

PSALM 90:3-4, 5-6, 12-13, 14 AND 17

You turn man back to dust,
saying, "Return, O children of men."
For a thousand years in your sight
are as yesterday, now that it is past,
or as a watch of the night.

You make an end of them in their sleep;
the next morning they are like the changing grass,
Which at dawn springs up anew,
but by evening wilts and fades.

IN EVERY AGE, O LORD, YOU HAVE BEEN OUR REFUGE.

when will you come?
how long, O Lord?

Teach us to number our days aright,
that we may gain wisdom of heart.
Return, O LORD! How long?
Have pity on your servants!

Thank you, Lord, for this new day; guide me in your ways

Fill us at daybreak with your kindness,
that we may shout for joy and gladness all our days.
And may the gracious care of the LORD our God be ours;
prosper the work of our hands for us!
Prosper the work of our hands!

2ND READING

PHILEMON 9-10, 12-17

I, Paul, an old man,
and now also a prisoner for Christ Jesus,
urge you on behalf of my child Onesimus,
whose father I have become in my imprisonment;
I am sending him, that is, my own heart, back to you.
I should have liked to retain him for myself,
so that he might serve me on your behalf
in my imprisonment for the gospel,
but I did not want to do anything without your consent,
so that the good you do might not be forced but voluntary.
Perhaps this is why he was away from you for a while,
that you might have him back forever,
no longer as a slave
but more than a slave, a brother,
beloved especially to me, but even more so to you,
as a man and in the Lord.
So if you regard me as a partner, welcome him as you would me.

Lk 14:25-33 GOSPEL

Great crowds were traveling with Jesus,
and he turned and addressed them,
"If anyone comes to me without hating his father and mother,
wife and children, brothers and sisters,
and even his own life,
he cannot be my disciple.
Whoever does not carry his own cross and come after me
cannot be my disciple.
Which of you wishing to construct a tower
does not first sit down and calculate the cost
to see if there is enough for its completion?
Otherwise, after laying the foundation
and finding himself unable to finish the work
the onlookers should laugh at him and say,
'This one began to build but did not have the resources to finish.'
Or what king marching into battle would not first sit down
and decide whether with ten thousand troops
he can successfully oppose another king
advancing upon him with twenty thousand troops?
But if not, while he is still far away,
he will send a delegation to ask for peace terms.
In the same way,
anyone of you who does not renounce all his possessions
cannot be my disciple."

TWENTY-FOURTH SUNDAY OF ORDINARY TIME 1ST READING

EX 32:7-11, 13-14

The LORD said to Moses,
"Go down at once to your people,
whom you brought out of the land of Egypt, for they have become depraved.
They have soon turned aside from the way I pointed out to them, making for themselves a molten calf and worshiping it,
sacrificing to it and crying out,
'This is your God, O Israel, who brought you out of the land of Egypt!'
"I see how stiff-necked this people is, " continued the LORD to Moses.
Let me alone, then, that my wrath may blaze up against them to consume them. Then I will make of you a great nation."

But Moses implored the LORD, his God, saying,
"Why, O LORD, should your wrath blaze up against your own people,
whom you brought out of the land of Egypt
with such great power and with so strong a hand?
Remember your servants Abraham, Isaac, and Israel,
and how you swore to them by your own self, saying,
'I will make your descendants as numerous as the stars in the sky;
and all this land that I promised,
I will give your descendants as their perpetual heritage.'"
So the LORD relented in the punishment
he had threatened to inflict on his people.

PSALM 51:3-4, 12-13, 17, 19

I WILL RISE AND GO TO MY FATHER.

Have mercy on me, O God, in your goodness;
in the greatness of your compassion wipe out my offense.
Thoroughly wash me from my guilt
and of my sin cleanse me.

A clean heart create for me, O God,
and a steadfast spirit renew within me.
Cast me not out from your presence,
and your Holy Spirit take not from me.

O Lord, open my lips,
and my mouth shall proclaim your praise.
My sacrifice, O God, is a contrite spirit;
a heart contrite and humbled, O God, you will not spurn.

Beloved:
I am grateful to him who has strengthened me, Christ Jesus our Lord,
because he considered me trustworthy
in appointing me to the ministry.
I was once a blasphemer and a persecutor and arrogant,
but I have been mercifully treated
because I acted out of ignorance in my unbelief.
Indeed, the grace of our Lord has been abundant,
along with the faith and love that are in Christ Jesus.
This saying is trustworthy and deserves full acceptance:
Christ Jesus came into the world to save sinners.
Of these I am the foremost.
But for that reason I was mercifully treated,
so that in me, as the foremost,
Christ Jesus might display all his patience as an example
for those who would come to believe in him for everlasting life.
To the king of ages, incorruptible, invisible, the only God,
honor and glory forever and ever. Amen.

2ND READING

1 TM 1:12-17

Luke 15:1-10 or luke 15: 1-32

GOSPEL

Tax collectors and sinners were all drawing near to listen to Jesus,
but the Pharisees and scribes began to complain, saying,
"This man welcomes sinners and eats with them."
So to them he addressed this parable.
"What man among you having a hundred sheep and losing one of them
would not leave the ninety-nine in the desert
and go after the lost one until he finds it?
And when he does find it,
he sets it on his shoulders with great joy
and, upon his arrival home,
he calls together his friends and neighbors and says to them,
'Rejoice with me because I have found my lost sheep.'
I tell you, in just the same way
there will be more joy in heaven over one sinner who repents
than over ninety-nine righteous people
who have no need of repentance.

"Or what woman having ten coins and losing one
would not light a lamp and sweep the house,
searching carefully until she finds it?
And when she does find it,
she calls together her friends and neighbors
and says to them,
'Rejoice with me because I have found the coin that I lost.'
In just the same way, I tell you,
there will be rejoicing among the angels of God
over one sinner who repents."

1ST READING

AMOS 8:4-7

TWENTY-FIFTH SUNDAY OF ORDINARY TIME

Hear this, you who trample upon the needy
and destroy the poor of the land!
"When will the new moon be over," you ask,
"that we may sell our grain,
and the sabbath, that we may display the wheat?
We will diminish the ephah,
add to the shekel,
and fix our scales for cheating!
We will buy the lowly for silver,
and the poor for a pair of sandals;
even the refuse of the wheat we will sell!"
The LORD has sworn by the pride of Jacob:
Never will I forget a thing they have done!

PSALM
113:1-2, 4-6, 7-8

Praise, you servants of the LORD,
praise the name of the LORD.
Blessed be the name of the LORD
both now and forever.

PRAISE THE LORD WHO LIFTS UP THE POOR. (OR ALLELUIA.)

High above all nations is the LORD;
above the heavens is his glory.
Who is like the LORD, our God, who is enthroned on high
and looks upon the heavens and the earth below?

He raises up the lowly from the dust;
from the dunghill he lifts up the poor
to seat them with princes,
with the princes of his own people.

2ND READING

1 TIMOTHY 2:1-8

Beloved:
First of all, I ask that supplications, prayers,
petitions, and thanksgivings be offered for everyone,
for kings and for all in authority,
that we may lead a quiet and tranquil life
in all devotion and dignity.
This is good and pleasing to God our savior,
who wills everyone to be saved
and to come to knowledge of the truth.
For there is one God.
There is also one mediator between God and men,
    the man Christ Jesus,
who gave himself as ransom for all.
This was the testimony at the proper time.
For this I was appointed preacher and apostle
– I am speaking the truth, I am not lying –,
teacher of the Gentiles in faith and truth.
It is my wish, then, that in every place the men should pray,
lifting up holy hands, without anger or argument.

GOSPEL

LUKE 16:10-13

OR LUKE 16: 1-13

Jesus said to his disciples:
"The person who is trustworthy in very small matters
is also trustworthy in great ones;
and the person who is dishonest in very small matters
is also dishonest in great ones.
If, therefore, you are not trustworthy with dishonest
wealth, who will trust you with true wealth?
If you are not trustworthy with what belongs to another,
who will give you what is yours?
No servant can serve two masters.
He will either hate one and love the other,
or be devoted to one and despise the other.
You cannot serve both God and mammon."

Thus says the LORD the God of hosts:
Woe to the complacent in Zion!
Lying upon beds of ivory,
stretched comfortably on their couches,
they eat lambs taken from the flock,
and calves from the stall!
Improvising to the music of the harp,
like David, they devise their own accompaniment.
They drink wine from bowls
and anoint themselves with the best oils;
yet they are not made ill by the collapse of Joseph!
Therefore, now they shall be the first to go into exile,
and their wanton revelry shall be done away with.

1ST READING

AMOS 6:1A, 4-7

TWENTY-SIXTH SUNDAY OF ORDINARY TIME

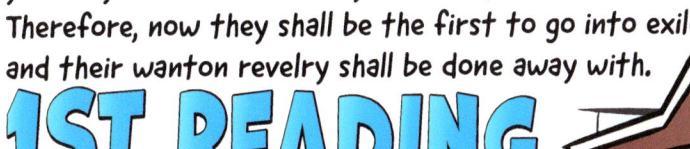

PRAISE THE LORD, MY SOUL!

PSALM 146:7, 8-9, 9-10

(OR ALLELUIA.)

Blessed he who keeps faith forever,
 secures justice for the oppressed,
 gives food to the hungry.
The LORD sets captives free.

The LORD gives sight to the blind;
 the LORD raises up those who were bowed down.
The LORD loves the just;
 the LORD protects strangers.

The fatherless and the widow he sustains,
 but the way of the wicked he thwarts.
The LORD shall reign forever;
 your God, O Zion, through all generations. Alleluia.

2ND READING

1 TIMOTHY 6:11-16

But you, man of God, pursue righteousness,
devotion, faith, love, patience, and gentleness.
Compete well for the faith.
Lay hold of eternal life, to which you were called
when you made the noble confession in the presence of many witnesses.
I charge you before God, who gives life to all things,
and before Christ Jesus,
who gave testimony under Pontius Pilate for the noble confession,
to keep the commandment without stain or reproach
until the appearance of our Lord Jesus Christ
that the blessed and only ruler
will make manifest at the proper time,
the King of kings and Lord of lords,
who alone has immortality, who dwells in unapproachable light,
and whom no human being has seen or can see.
To him be honor and eternal power. Amen.

GOSPEL Luke 16:19–31

Jesus said to the Pharisees:
"There was a rich man who dressed in purple garments and fine linen
and dined sumptuously each day.
And lying at his door was a poor man named Lazarus, covered with sores,

who would gladly have eaten his fill of the scraps
that fell from the rich man's table.
Dogs even used to come and lick his sores.
When the poor man died,
he was carried away by angels to the bosom of Abraham.
The rich man also died and was buried,
and from the netherworld, where he was in torment,
he raised his eyes and saw Abraham far off
and Lazarus at his side.
And he cried out, 'Father Abraham, have pity on me.
Send Lazarus to dip the tip of his finger in water and cool my tongue,

for I am suffering torment in these flames.'
Abraham replied,
'My child, remember that you received
what was good during your lifetime
while Lazarus likewise received what was bad;
but now he is comforted here, whereas you are tormented.

Moreover, between us and you a great chasm is established
to prevent anyone from crossing who might wish to go
from our side to yours or from your side to ours.'
He said, 'Then I beg you, father,
send him to my father's house, for I have five brothers,
so that he may warn them,
lest they too come to this place of torment.'
But Abraham replied, 'They have Moses and the prophets.
Let them listen to them.'
He said, 'Oh no, father Abraham,
but if someone from the dead goes to them, they will repent.'
Then Abraham said, 'If they will not listen to Moses and the prophets,
neither will they be persuaded if someone should rise from the dead.'"

TWENTY-SEVENTH SUNDAY OF ORDINARY TIME

1ST READING

HABAKKUK 1:2-3; 2:2-4

How long, O LORD? I cry for help
but you do not listen!
I cry out to you, "Violence!"
but you do not intervene.
Why do you let me see ruin;
why must I look at misery?
Destruction and violence are before me;
there is strife, and clamorous discord.
Then the LORD answered me and said:
Write down the vision clearly upon the tablets,
so that one can read it readily.
For the vision still has its time,
presses on to fulfillment, and will not disappoint;
if it delays, wait for it,
it will surely come, it will not be late.
The rash one has no integrity;
but the just one, because of his faith, shall live.

Come, let us sing joyfully to the LORD;
let us acclaim the rock of our salvation.
Let us come into his presence with thanksgiving;
let us joyfully sing psalms to him.

Come, let us bow down in worship;
let us kneel before the LORD who made us.
For he is our God,
and we are the people he shepherds, the flock he guides.

PSALM 95:1-2, 6-7, 8-9

Oh, that today you would hear his voice:
"Harden not your hearts as at Meribah,
as in the day of Massah in the desert,
Where your fathers tempted me;
they tested me though they had seen my works."

IF TODAY YOU HEAR HIS VOICE, HARDEN NOT YOUR HEARTS

2ND READING

2 TM 1:6-8, 13-14

Beloved:
I remind you, to stir into flame
the gift of God that you have through the imposition of my hands.
For God did not give us a spirit of cowardice
but rather of power and love and self-control.
So do not be ashamed of your testimony to our Lord,
nor of me, a prisoner for his sake;
but bear your share of hardship for the gospel
with the strength that comes from God.

Take as your norm the sound words that you heard from me,
in the faith and love that are in Christ Jesus.
Guard this rich trust with the help of the Holy Spirit
that dwells within us.

LUKE 17:5-10

GOSPEL

The apostles said to the Lord, "Increase our faith."
The Lord replied,
"If you have faith the size of a mustard seed,
you would say to this mulberry tree,
'Be uprooted and planted in the sea,' and it would obey you.

"Who among you would say to your servant
who has just come in from plowing or tending sheep in the field,
'Come here immediately and take your place at table'?
Would he not rather say to him,
'Prepare something for me to eat.
Put on your apron and wait on me while I eat and drink.
You may eat and drink when I am finished'?
Is he grateful to that servant because he did what was
commanded?So should it be with you.
When you have done all you have been commanded,
say, 'We are unprofitable servants;
we have done what we were obliged to do.'"

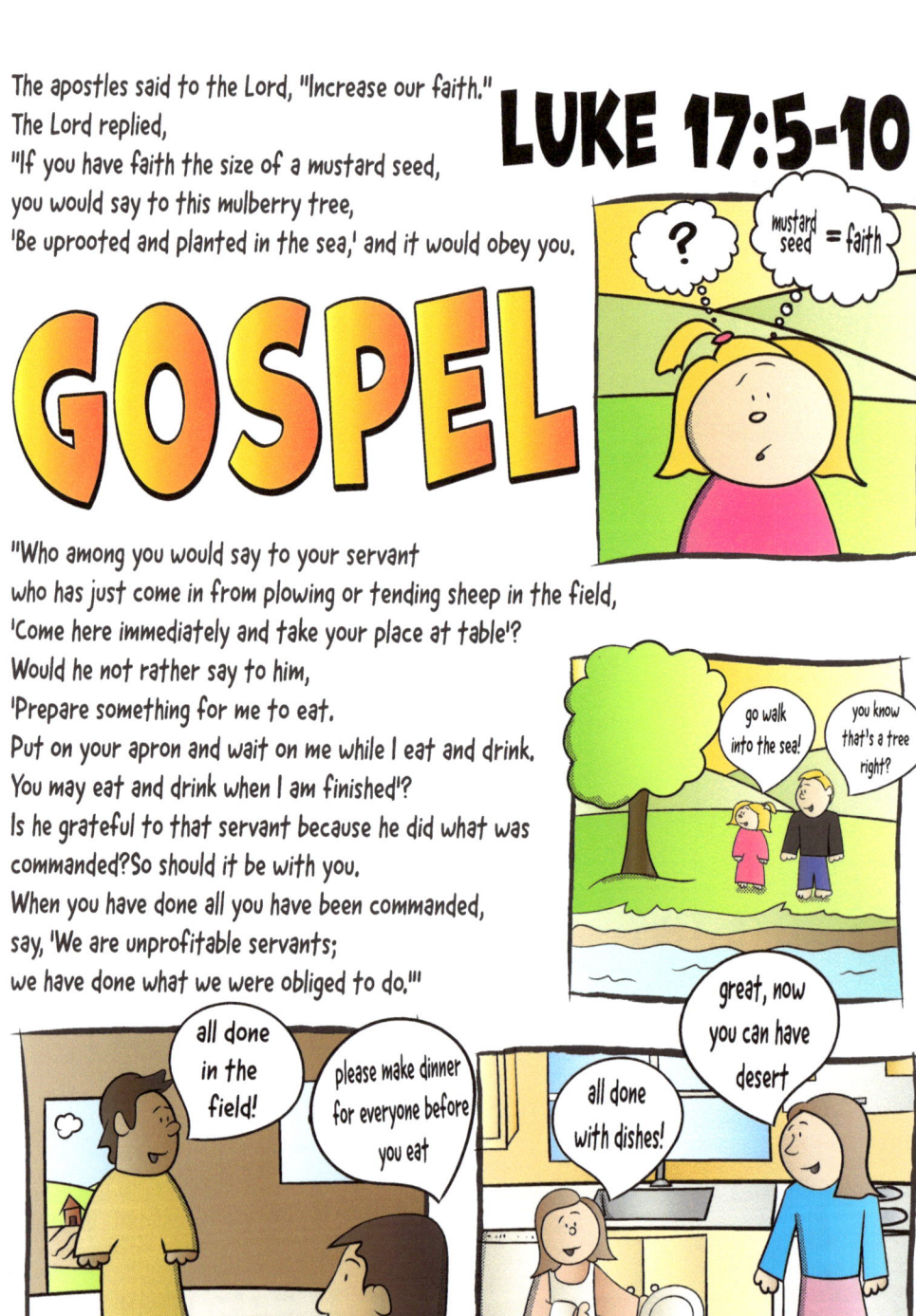

Naaman went down and plunged into the Jordan seven times
at the word of Elisha, the man of God.
His flesh became again like the flesh of a little child,
and he was clean of his leprosy.

2 KGS 5:14-17

Naaman returned with his whole retinue to the man of God.
On his arrival he stood before Elisha and said,
"Now I know that there is no God in all the
earth, except in Israel.
Please accept a gift from your servant."

TWENTY-EIGHTH SUNDAY OF ORDINARY TIME

Elisha replied, "As the LORD lives whom I serve, I will not take it;"
and despite Naaman's urging, he still refused.
Naaman said: "If you will not accept,
please let me, your servant, have two mule-loads of earth,
for I will no longer offer holocaust or sacrifice
to any other god except to the LORD."

PSALM
98:1, 2-3, 3-4

Sing to the LORD a new song,
for he has done wondrous deeds;
His right hand has won victory for him,
his holy arm.

The LORD has made his salvation known:
in the sight of the nations he has revealed his justice.
He has remembered his kindness and his faithfulness
toward the house of Israel.

All the ends of the earth have seen
the salvation by our God.
Sing joyfully to the LORD, all you lands;
break into song; sing praise.

THE LORD HAS REVEALED TO THE NATIONS HIS SAVING POWER.

Beloved: Remember Jesus Christ, raised from the dead, a descendant of David: such is my gospel, for which I am suffering, even to the point of chains, like a criminal. But the word of God is not chained. Therefore, I bear with everything for the sake of those who are chosen, so that they too may obtain the salvation that is in Christ Jesus, together with eternal glory. This saying is trustworthy:

2ND READING

2 Timothy 2:8–13

If we have died with him
we shall also live with him;
if we persevere
we shall also reign with him.
But if we deny him
he will deny us.
If we are unfaithful
he remains faithful,
for he cannot deny himself.

GOSPEL Luke 17: 11-19

As Jesus continued his journey to Jerusalem, he traveled through Samaria and Galilee. As he was entering a village, ten lepers met him. They stood at a distance from him and raised their voices, saying,

"Jesus, Master! Have pity on us!" And when he saw them, he said, "Go show yourselves to the priests." As they were going they were cleansed. And one of them, realizing he had been healed, returned, glorifying God in a loud voice;

and he fell at the feet of Jesus and thanked him. He was a Samaritan. Jesus said in reply, "Ten were cleansed, were they not? Where are the other nine? Has none but this foreigner returned to give thanks to God?" Then he said to him, "Stand up and go; your faith has saved you."

TWENTY-NINTH SUNDAY OF ORDINARY TIME

In those days, Amalek came and waged war against Israel.
Moses, therefore, said to Joshua,
"Pick out certain men,
and tomorrow go out and engage Amalek in battle.
I will be standing on top of the hill
with the staff of God in my hand."
So Joshua did as Moses told him:
he engaged Amalek in battle
after Moses had climbed to the top of the hill with Aaron and Hur.
As long as Moses kept his hands raised up,
Israel had the better of the fight,
but when he let his hands rest,
Amalek had the better of the fight.
Moses'hands, however, grew tired;
so they put a rock in place for him to sit on.
Meanwhile Aaron and Hur supported his hands,
one on one side and one on the other,
so that his hands remained steady till sunset.
And Joshua mowed down Amalek and his people
with the edge of the sword.

1ST READING

EXODUS 17:8-13

OUR HELP IS FROM THE LORD, WHO MADE HEAVEN AND EARTH.

PSALM 121:1-2, 3-4, 5-6, 7-8

I lift up my eyes toward the mountains;
whence shall help come to me?
My help is from the LORD,
who made heaven and earth.

May he not suffer your foot to slip;
may he slumber not who guards you:
indeed he neither slumbers nor sleeps,
the guardian of Israel.

The LORD is your guardian; the LORD is your shade;
he is beside you at your right hand.
The sun shall not harm you by day,
nor the moon by night.

The LORD will guard you from all evil;
he will guard your life.
The LORD will guard your coming and your going,
both now and forever.

Beloved:
Remain faithful to what you have learned and believed, because you know from whom you learned it, and that from infancy you have known the sacred Scriptures, which are capable of giving you wisdom for salvation through faith in Christ Jesus. All Scripture is inspired by God and is useful for teaching, for refutation, for correction, and for training in righteousness, so that one who belongs to God may be competent, equipped for every good work.

2ND READING

2 TIMOTHY 3:14-4:2

I charge you in the presence of God and of Christ Jesus, who will judge the living and the dead, and by his appearing and his kingly power: proclaim the word; be persistent whether it is convenient or inconvenient; convince, reprimand, encourage through all patience and teaching.

GOSPEL

Luke 18:1-8

Jesus told his disciples a parable about the necessity for them to pray always without becoming weary. He said, "There was a judge in a certain town who neither feared God nor respected any human being. And a widow in that town used to come to him and say, 'Render a just decision for me against my adversary.' For a long time the judge was unwilling, but eventually he thought, 'While it is true that I neither fear God nor respect any human being, because this widow keeps bothering me I shall deliver a just decision for her lest she finally come and strike me.'" The Lord said, "Pay attention to what the dishonest judge says. Will not God then secure the rights of his chosen ones who call out to him day and night? Will he be slow to answer them? I tell you, he will see to it that justice is done for them speedily. But when the Son of Man comes, will he find faith on earth?"

THIRTIETH SUNDAY OF ORDINARY TIME

SIR 35:12-14, 16-18

The LORD is a God of justice,
who knows no favorites.
Though not unduly partial toward the weak,
yet he hears the cry of the oppressed.
The Lord is not deaf to the wail of the orphan,
nor to the widow when she pours out her complaint.
The one who serves God willingly is heard;
his petition reaches the heavens.
The prayer of the lowly pierces the clouds;
it does not rest till it reaches its goal,
nor will it withdraw till the Most High responds,
judges justly and affirms the right,
and the Lord will not delay.

THE LORD HEARS THE CRY OF THE POOR.

PSALM 134:2-3, 17-18, 19, 23

I will bless the LORD at all times;
his praise shall be ever in my mouth.
Let my soul glory in the LORD;
the lowly will hear me and be glad.

The LORD confronts the evildoers,
to destroy remembrance of them from the earth.
When the just cry out, the Lord hears them,
and from all their distress he rescues them.

The LORD is close to the brokenhearted;
and those who are crushed in spirit he saves.
The LORD redeems the lives of his servants;
no one incurs guilt who takes refuge in him.

2ND READING

Beloved:
I am already being poured out like a libation,
and the time of my departure is at hand.
I have competed well; I have finished the race;
I have kept the faith.
From now on the crown of righteousness awaits me,
which the Lord, the just judge,
will award to me on that day, and not only to me,
but to all who have longed for his appearance.

At my first defense no one appeared on my behalf,
but everyone deserted me.
May it not be held against them!
But the Lord stood by me and gave me strength,
so that through me the proclamation might be completed
and all the Gentiles might hear it.
And I was rescued from the lion's mouth.
The Lord will rescue me from every evil threat
and will bring me safe to his heavenly kingdom.
To him be glory forever and ever. Amen.

2 Timothy 4:6-8, 16-18

GOSPEL Luke 18:9–14

Jesus addressed this parable
to those who were convinced of their own righteousness
and despised everyone else.
"Two people went up to the temple area to pray;
one was a Pharisee and the other was a tax collector.
The Pharisee took up his position and spoke this prayer to himself,
'O God, I thank you that I am not like the rest of humanity --
greedy, dishonest, adulterous -- or even like this tax collector.
I fast twice a week, and I pay tithes on my whole income.'
But the tax collector stood off at a distance
and would not even raise his eyes to heaven
but beat his breast and prayed,
'O God, be merciful to me a sinner.'
I tell you, the latter went home justified, not the former;
for whoever exalts himself will be humbled,
and the one who humbles himself will be exalted."

THIRTY-FIRST SUNDAY OF ORDINARY TIME 1ST READING

WISDOM 11:22-12:2

Before the LORD the whole universe is as a grain from a balance
or a drop of morning dew come down upon the earth.
But you have mercy on all, because you can do all things;
and you overlook people's sins that they may repent.
For you love all things that are
and loathe nothing that you have made;
for what you hated, you would not have fashioned.
And how could a thing remain, unless you willed it;
or be preserved, had it not been called forth by you?
But you spare all things, because they are yours,
O LORD and lover of souls,
for your imperishable spirit is in all things!
Therefore you rebuke offenders little by little,
warn them and remind them of the sins they are committing,
that they may abandon their wickedness and believe in you, O LORD!

I WILL PRAISE YOUR NAME FOR EVER, MY KING AND MY GOD.

I will extol you, O my God and King,
and I will bless your name forever and ever.
Every day will I bless you,
and I will praise your name forever and ever.

PSALM 145:1-2, 8-9, 10-11, 13, 14

The LORD is gracious and merciful,
slow to anger and of great kindness.
The LORD is good to all
and compassionate toward all his works.

Let all your works give you thanks, O LORD,
and let your faithful ones bless you.
Let them discourse of the glory of your kingdom
and speak of your might.

The LORD is faithful in all his words
and holy in all his works.
The LORD lifts up all who are falling
and raises up all who are bowed down.

2ND READING
2 Thes 1:11–2:2

Brothers and sisters:
We always pray for you,
that our God may make you worthy of his calling
and powerfully bring to fulfillment every good purpose
and every effort of faith,
that the name of our Lord Jesus may be glorified in you,
and you in him,
in accord with the grace of our God and Lord Jesus Christ.

We ask you, brothers and sisters, with regard to the coming of our Lord Jesus Christ and our assembling with him, not to be shaken out of your minds suddenly, or to be alarmed either by a "spirit," or by an oral statement, or by a letter allegedly from us to the effect that the day of the Lord is at hand.

GOSPEL

Luke 19:1-10

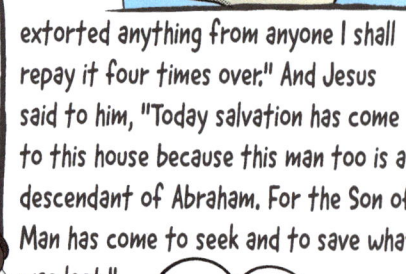

At that time, Jesus came to Jericho and intended to pass through the town. Now a man there named Zacchaeus, who was a chief tax collector and also a wealthy man, was seeking to see who Jesus was; but he could not see him because of the crowd, for he was short in stature. So he ran ahead and climbed a sycamore tree in order to see Jesus, who was about to pass that way. When he reached the place, Jesus looked up and said, "Zacchaeus, come down quickly, for today I must stay at your house." And he came down quickly and received him with joy. When they all saw this, they began to grumble, saying, "He has gone to stay at the house of a sinner." But Zacchaeus stood there and said to the Lord, "Behold, half of my possessions, Lord, I shall give to the poor, and if I have extorted anything from anyone I shall repay it four times over." And Jesus said to him, "Today salvation has come to this house because this man too is a descendant of Abraham. For the Son of Man has come to seek and to save what was lost."

THIRTY-SECOND SUNDAY OF ORDINARY TIME

1ST READING 2 MACCABEES 7:1-2, 9-14

It happened that seven brothers with their mother were arrested and tortured with whips and scourges by the king, to force them to eat pork in violation of God's law. One of the brothers, speaking for the others, said: "What do you expect to achieve by questioning us? We are ready to die rather than transgress the laws of our ancestors."

At the point of death he said:
"You accursed fiend, you are depriving us of this present life, but the King of the world will raise us up to live again forever.
It is for his laws that we are dying."

After him the third suffered their cruel sport.
He put out his tongue at once when told to do so, and bravely held out his hands, as he spoke these noble words:
"It was from Heaven that I received these;
for the sake of his laws I disdain them;
from him I hope to receive them again."
Even the king and his attendants marveled at the young man's courage, because he regarded his sufferings as nothing.

After he had died, they tortured and maltreated the fourth brother in the same way. When he was near death, he said, "It is my choice to die at the hands of men with the hope God gives of being raised up by him; but for you, there will be no resurrection to life."

PSALM

17:1, 5-6, 8, 15

LORD, WHEN YOUR GLORY APPEARS, MY JOY WILL BE FULL.

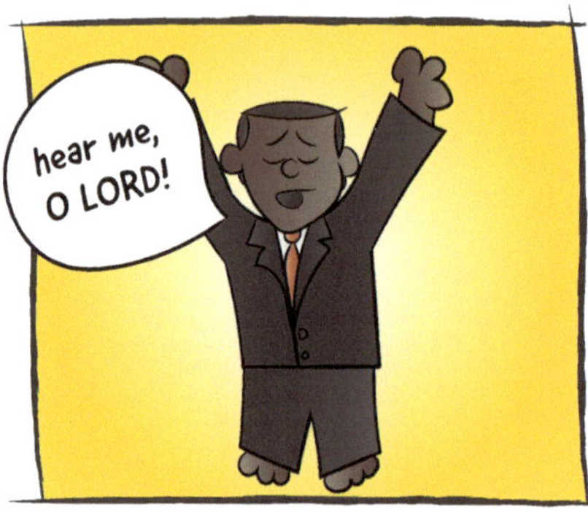

Hear, O LORD, a just suit;
attend to my outcry;
hearken to my prayer from lips without deceit.

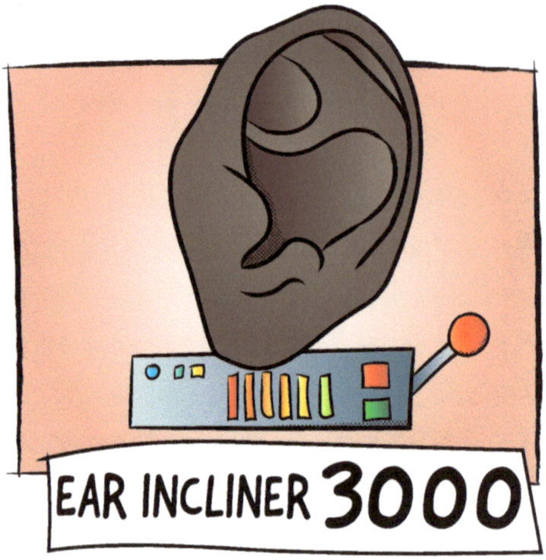

My steps have been steadfast in your paths,
my feet have not faltered.
I call upon you, for you will answer me, O God;
incline your ear to me; hear my word.

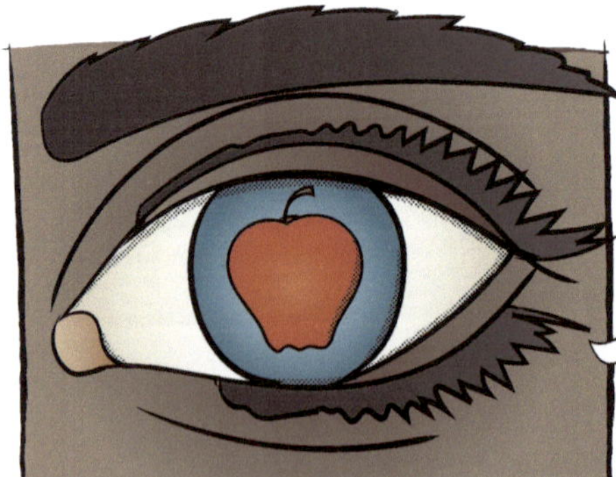

Keep me as the apple of your eye,
hide me in the shadow of your wings.
But I in justice shall behold your face;
on waking I shall be content in your presence.

2ND READING
2 Thes 2:16–3:5

Brothers and sisters:
May our Lord Jesus Christ himself and God our Father,
who has loved us and given us everlasting encouragement
and good hope through his grace, encourage your hearts
and strengthen them in every good deed and word.

Finally, brothers and sisters, pray for us,
so that the word of the Lord may speed forward and be glorified,
as it did among you,
and that we may be delivered from perverse and wicked people,
for not all have faith.
But the Lord is faithful;
he will strengthen you and guard you from the evil one.
We are confident of you in the Lord that what we instruct you,
you are doing and will continue to do.
May the Lord direct your hearts to the love of God
and to the endurance of Christ.

Some Sadducees, those who deny that there is a resurrection, came forward.

GOSPEL

Luke 20:27, 34-38

or Lk 20:27-38

Jesus said to them,
"The children of this age marry and remarry;
but those who are deemed worthy to attain to the coming age
and to the resurrection of the dead
neither marry nor are given in marriage.
They can no longer die,
for they are like angels;
and they are the children of God
because they are the ones who will rise.
That the dead will rise
even Moses made known in the passage about the bush,
when he called out 'Lord, '
the God of Abraham, the God of Isaac, and the God of Jacob;
and he is not God of the dead, but of the living,
for to him all are alive."

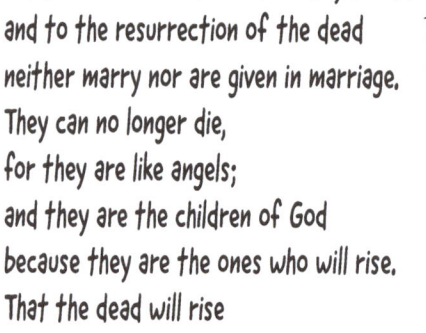

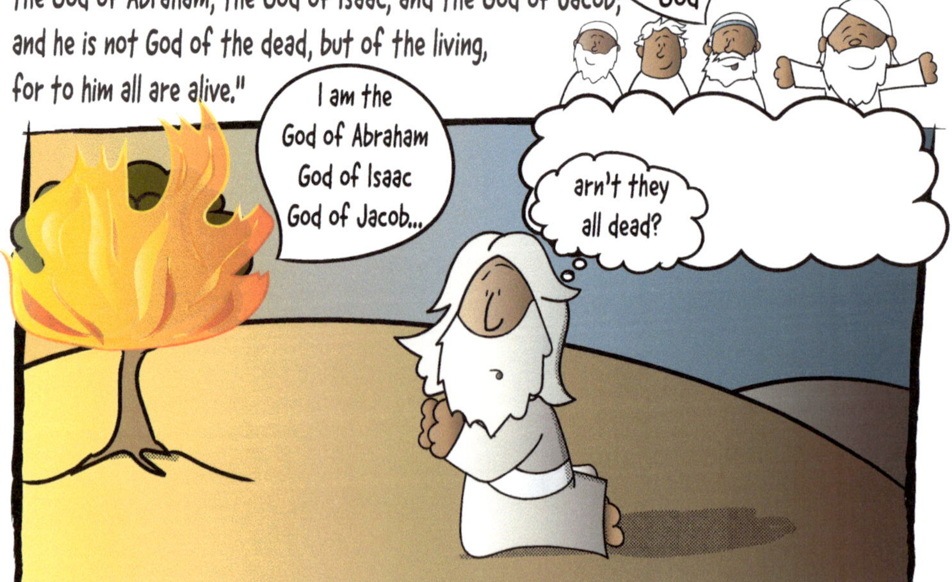

THIRTY-THIRD SUNDAY OF ORDINARY TIME

1ST READING

Lo, the day is coming, blazing like an oven,
when all the proud and all evildoers will be stubble,
and the day that is coming will set them on fire,
leaving them neither root nor branch,
says the LORD of hosts.
But for you who fear my name, there will arise
the sun of justice with its healing rays.

Malachi 3:19–20a

THE LORD COMES TO RULE THE EARTH WITH JUSTICE.

PSALM 98:5-6, 7-8, 9

Sing praise to the LORD with the harp,
with the harp and melodious song.
With trumpets and the sound of the horn
sing joyfully before the King, the LORD..

Let the sea and what fills it resound,
the world and those who dwell in it;
let the rivers clap their hands,
the mountains shout with them for joy.

Before the LORD, for he comes,
for he comes to rule the earth,
he will rule the world with justice
and the peoples with equity.

2ND READING

2 Thes 3:7-12

Brothers and sisters:
You know how one must imitate us.
For we did not act in a disorderly way among you,
nor did we eat food received free from anyone.
On the contrary, in toil and drudgery, night and day
we worked, so as not to burden any of you.
Not that we do not have the right.
Rather, we wanted to present ourselves as
a model for you, so that you might imitate us.
In fact, when we were with you,
we instructed you that if anyone was
unwilling to work, neither should that one eat.
We hear that some are conducting themselves
among you in a disorderly way,
by not keeping busy but minding the business of others.
Such people we instruct and urge in the Lord Jesus Christ to work quietly
and to eat their own food.

While some people were speaking about how the temple was adorned with costly stones and votive offerings, Jesus said, "All that you see here--the days will come when there will not be left a stone upon another stone that will not be thrown down."

GOSPEL

Luke 21:5-19

Then they asked him,
"Teacher, when will this happen?
And what sign will there be when all these things are about to happen?"
He answered,
"See that you not be deceived,
for many will come in my name, saying,
'I am he,' and 'The time has come.'
Do not follow them!
When you hear of wars and insurrections,
do not be terrified; for such things must happen first,
but it will not immediately be the end."
Then he said to them,
"Nation will rise against nation, and kingdom against kingdom.
There will be powerful earthquakes, famines, and plagues
from place to place;
and awesome sights and mighty signs will come from the sky.

"Before all this happens, however, they will seize and persecute you, they will hand you over to the synagogues and to prisons, and they will have you led before kings and governors because of my name. It will lead to your giving testimony. Remember, you are not to prepare your defense beforehand, for I myself shall give you a wisdom in speaking that all your adversaries will be powerless to resist or refute. You will even be handed over by parents, brothers, relatives, and friends, and they will put some of you to death. You will be hated by all because of my name, but not a hair on your head will be destroyed. By your perseverance you will secure your lives."

THE SOLEMNITY OF OUR LORD JESUS CHRIST, KING OF THE UNIVERSE

1ST READING 2 Sm 5:1-3

In those days, all the tribes of Israel came to David in Hebron and said:
"Here we are, your bone and your flesh.
In days past, when Saul was our king,
it was you who led the Israelites out and brought them back.
And the LORD said to you,
'You shall shepherd my people Israel
and shall be commander of Israel.'"
When all the elders of Israel came to David in Hebron,
King David made an agreement with them there before the LORD,
and they anointed him king of Israel.

PSALM 122:1-2, 3-4, 4-5

LET US GO REJOICING TO THE HOUSE OF THE LORD.

I rejoiced because they said to me,
"We will go up to the house of the LORD."
And now we have set foot
within your gates, O Jerusalem.

Jerusalem, built as a city
with compact unity.
To it the tribes go up,
the tribes of the LORD.

According to the decree for Israel,
to give thanks to the name of the LORD.
In it are set up judgment seats,
seats for the house of David.

Col 1:12-20

2ND READING

Brothers and sisters:
Let us give thanks to the Father,
who has made you fit to share
in the inheritance of the holy ones in light.
He delivered us from the power of darkness
and transferred us to the kingdom of his beloved Son,
in whom we have redemption, the forgiveness of sins.

He is the image of the invisible God,
the firstborn of all creation.
For in him were created all things in heaven and on earth,
the visible and the invisible,
whether thrones or dominions or principalities or powers;
all things were created through him and for him.
He is before all things,
and in him all things hold together.
He is the head of the body, the church.
He is the beginning, the firstborn from the dead,
that in all things he himself might be preeminent.
For in him all the fullness was pleased to dwell,
and through him to reconcile all things for him,
making peace by the blood of his cross
through him, whether those on earth or those in heaven.

GOSPEL

The rulers sneered at Jesus and said,
"He saved others, let him save himself
if he is the chosen one, the Christ of God."
Even the soldiers jeered at him.
As they approached to offer him wine they called out,
"If you are King of the Jews, save yourself."
Above him there was an inscription that read,
"This is the King of the Jews."

Luke 23:35-43

Now one of the criminals hanging there reviled Jesus, saying,
"Are you not the Christ?
Save yourself and us."
The other, however, rebuking him, said in reply,
"Have you no fear of God,
for you are subject to the same condemnation?
And indeed, we have been condemned justly,
for the sentence we received corresponds to our crimes,
but this man has done nothing criminal."
Then he said,
"Jesus, remember me when you come into your kingdom."
He replied to him,
"Amen, I say to you,
today you will be with me in Paradise."

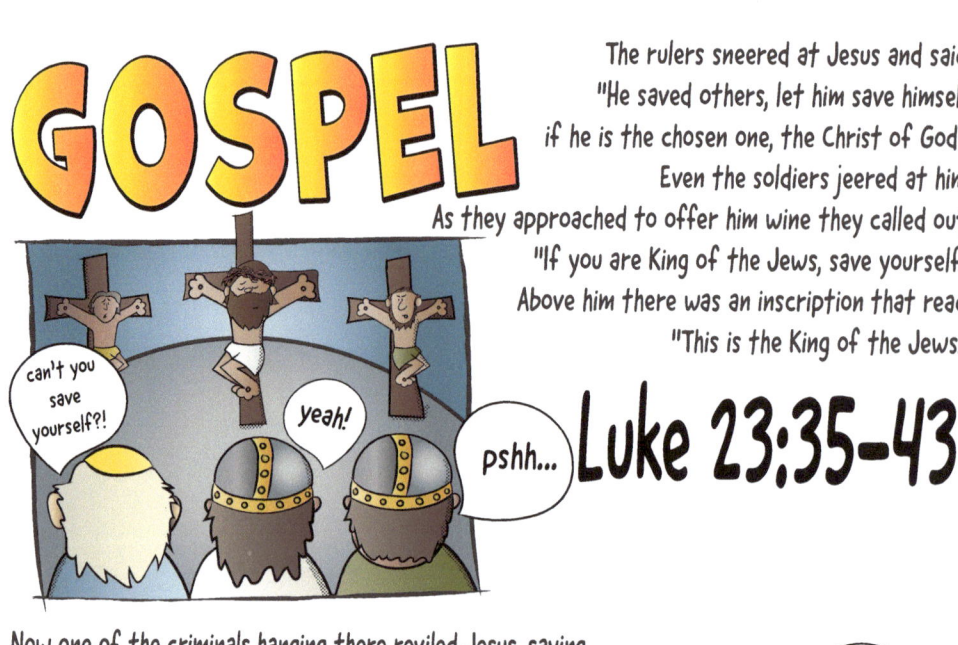

created by kids for kids

The Dickinson family—Gabbi, Grace, Joseph, Ann Marie, Elijah, and Catherine, along with their mom, Tiffany—discuss the scriptures and create drawings to tell the stories. Their dad, Kevin, sends them to McAfee Studios, who creates the colorful story panels. Monsignor David, our spiritual director then approves for the eventual Imprimatur from Bishop Taylor of our home Dioceses.

About the Dickinson Family

We are a family of 9 who loves our Faith & our Family. When we are not running to and from Sports, Dance and other activities, we love to spend time with each other, our friends and church community.

Tiffany and Kevin Dickinson, parents - Kids' Assistants
Gabrielle, 16, (Business Manager)
Grace, 14, (Director of Sales)
Joseph, 13, (Head Kids Illustrator)
Ann Marie, 11,(Digital Marketing Manager)
Elijah, 10, (Formatting)
Catherine, 6, (Director of Coloring Books)
Xavier, New Born, (Boss Baby)

SPECIAL THANKS

Travis McAfee - Illustrator
Msgr. David Lesieur - Spiritual Advisor
Our Sunday Visitor - Innovation Challenge

www.ingramcontent.com/pod-product-compliance
Lightning Source LLC
LaVergne TN
LVHW010018070426
835512LV00001B/8
9781959127017